T0165514

Achieving peace, equality and a healthy environment

Achieving peace, equality and a healthy environment

Dr. Jerome Teelucksingh

authorHOUSE®

AuthorHouse™
1663 Liberty Drive
Bloomington, IN 47403
www.authorhouse.com
Phone: 1-800-839-8640

First published by AuthorHouse   11/23/2011

ISBN: 978-1-4634-4218-7 (sc)
ISBN: 978-1-4634-4217-0 (ebk)

Printed in the United States of America

Dedicated to all who contribute to a better world

Table of Contents

Preface

"**I** know the concept explaining the formation of rain but show me the law that says millions of human beings must suffer from malnutrition or live without clean water. I understand the biological explanation that humans need air to survive but show me the law which states that humans must be forced to live in slums and polluted areas. I know the law of nature where some animals hunt each other to survive but show me the law that proves human beings must kill, injure or shoot fellow humans. I know the scientific law of gravity but please explain to me which laws state that gender inequality, murder and child abuse must exist." This was my opening statement I had posed to my undergraduate History class of 70 students in 2009. They were all confused. They did not expect these questions on the first day of a supposedly boring History class that was restricted to the past! I asked another question—Is it possible to create a world without poverty, injustice, sadness, racism or pollution? They said no. I wanted these students to understand that WE can find solutions for problems that WE created. After class they began talking amongst themselves and with students from other Departments and faculties. I wanted them to be empowered to chart a new path and make history!

We are all searching for answers. The scientist is searching for a cure for a disease and the mathematician is searching for a solution to a problem. A child will spend hours searching for a lost toy or suitable places for the final pieces in a puzzle. We know the frustration of searching and the disappointment of not finding something.

We argue and debate over land ownership and the superiority of ethnicity, religion, political ideology, gender, class and caste. The result is that nobody is fully empowered. Why bother with these issues when millions of human lives are poor, oppressed, suffering, hungry and dying? On a daily basis in developing countries, millions of persons confront unemployment and oppressive political regimes. On a daily basis many persons painfully endure civil wars, illiteracy, overpopulation, infectious diseases, corruption, desertification, uncontrolled crime, a deplorable health care system and a lack of clean water. In many developing countries, the debt burdens deplete already scarce human and material resources.

In 1999, the revival of the observance of International Men's Day (IMD) signaled a watershed in the global men's movement. The date for International Men's Day was chosen to honor my dad, a retired Presbyterian minister, who resides in Trinidad and Tobago in the West Indies. His birthday is on 19th November and the day is also significant because on 19 November 1989, the football (soccer) team from my country, in its quest to qualify for the World Cup, united the citizens.

Despite its origins, this version of IMD is not about religious conversion, promoting religion, condemning cultures, eradicating capitalism, or praising soccer (football). A slow start and a small audience at the observance in 1999 would have been an ominous sign that this effort would be stillborn. Fortunately, the spark was kept burning and the explosion of IMD during 2008 and 2009 shocked many critics. It is a pleasant surprise to see that this seed had blossomed and bore fruit. Yes, IMD is not confined to a gender perspective. It has easily transcended cultural and language barriers. Furthermore, IMD observances were not limited to any particular class, disability, country, gender, ethnicity, religion, age or occupation. I never expected that International Men's Day would generate high levels of enthusiasm, understanding and cooperation.

There is need to also acknowledge the pioneering efforts of persons and groups before 1999 who attempted to formulate a day for men. The real heroes and heroines are the humble persons around the globe who have promoted IMD and demonstrated dedication and sacrifice. They are the ones to be honored. I'm grateful to all who assisted with advice, suggestions and recommendations. The priceless inputs of these persons were lifelines which contributed to the success of International Men's Day. Their contribution was the valuable lifeblood which kept IMD alive.

Their concerns are genuine and the common bond uniting these coordinators of IMD is their belief in individuals deciding to change their lives. The mission of these coordinators has rescued numerous individuals from the depths of destruction and despair. They are striving for gender equality and patiently attempt to remove the negative images and the stigma associated with men in our society.

Every year, *TIME* magazine, based in the United States, chooses an individual or group who has shaped and influenced our world. The selected person (s) would grace the front covers of the magazine and be dubbed 'Person of the Year.' Undoubtedly, the IMD coordinators and supporters deserve the honor and recognition of not only 'Persons of the Year' but 'Persons of the Day' and 'Persons of the Week'. This is because they have been keeping International Men's Day alive every day, every week and every month. They deserve this recognition and I salute everyone involved in this worldwide effort of co-operation and communication. They have built and carefully maintained a solid human infrastructure which connects individuals from around the globe.

Sympathizers and supporters are not seeking fifteen minutes of fame. They are part of IMD because they are aware of the long-term beneficial effects on society. They have helped re-define human relationships. Their loyalty and dedication are the vital engines of this movement. They have talent, experience and expertise which they willingly share with others. Their successes are obvious from the fact that each year there has been a steady increase in observances. These coordinators have been ably assisted by men's organizations, women's groups, gender departments at universities and individuals who have annually joined in similar ventures to celebrate International Men's Day. I appeal to individuals and organizations to take a bold step and decide to be coordinators or hold annual observances of International Men's Day on 19th November.

It is a commendable effort by these willing coordinators and volunteers. They are ensuring the continuous growth of this exciting phase of International Men's Day to create a better today and tomorrow. As International Men's Day continues to grow, the voices of the critics become more distant. As IMD emerges in more states and nations, the comments by doubters become less significant.

The annual observance of International Men's Day on November 19th indicates a deep concern for the numerous problems plaguing our families and by extension our society. It is annually observed by both men and women who support the effort to reform and save the troubled, help the dysfunctional and promote positive role models in our society. Celebrating International Men's Day will ultimately produce responsible and caring fathers, husbands and sons.

Trinidad and Tobago
West Indies
2011.

Introduction

Supporters, coordinators and participants of International Men's Day have been trying to embrace everyone, offer different perspectives and experiment with new ideas. This is evident from the Day's 6 Objectives—

- To promote positive male role models; not just movie stars and sports men but everyday, working class men who are living decent, honest lives.
- To celebrate men's positive contributions to society, community, family, marriage, child care and to the environment.
- To focus on men's health and well-being; social, emotional, physical and spiritual.
- To highlight discrimination against males; in areas of social services, social attitudes and expectations, and law.
- To improve gender relations and promote gender equality.
- To create a safer, better world; where people can be safe and grow to reach their full potential.

These Objectives might appear as impossible tasks. Promoters of IMD must **never** compromise the Day's 6 Objectives and be always cautious of responding to critics who are intent on creating confusion. Supporters, promoters and coordinators should see themselves as protectors and keepers of the 6 Objectives of International Men's Day. These Objectives are self-explanatory and transparent. This does not mean that participants, observers and coordinators are dreamers and living in a fantasy world. We are fully aware of the reality and the state of the world. And, we intend to do all within our power to genuinely improve and enhance this reality for the present and future generations.

The celebration of International Men's Day includes promoting solidarity and developing wholesome individuals. Such developments are badly needed in today's wounded communities which reveal scars due to hate and ignorance. The conflict among men, women and children must cease and the healing must begin.

Observers of IMD must try to convince non-believers of equality and those who shun peace, of the need for a new way of thinking and interacting with others. Even though I will be using terms as 'equality', 'freedom', and 'justice' it is difficult to decide on one acceptable meaning for each of these words. For some persons, freedom could entail being allowed to criticize the government and dress differently. The government might believe that a jail term of fifty years is justice for a guilty murderer. Is it justice for the victim and the victim's family? How can the poor boast of freedom? How can a democratic country allow racism, corruption and inequality to exist? Is it freedom if you have the right to vote but do not have access to proper health care?

Freedom of speech, opinion and expression are crucial in any democracy. But this freedom has its boundaries. Any comments and criticisms will allow the promoters and supporters of IMD to improve our efforts, reshape strategies and reassess goals. We live in a constantly changing society with diverse voices. Thus, we must expect debates and different views on values, religion, gender, political ideology, morals, ethics and behavior. Which version of democracy is the most suitable for a country? Who will decide what is right and wrong? What or who will be the yardstick to measure morals? Should the laws of a country decide on the behaviour or freedom of its citizens? Should traditional value systems be regularly replaced by new values? Will our actions decide our fate after death? Is religion improving society? Is it useless to attempt to change society? Can one person or group create permanent, positive changes? Should the decisions of the majority influence the minority? How can the voices of the minority be heard? Should we accept inequalities and injustices? Can we truly celebrate differences and diversity? Will permanent peace ever be achieved? In the following chapters I have attempted to answer some of the questions, asked more questions, offered suggestions and shared ideas. Most of these writings have been published in the journal—*In Search of Fatherhood*. Illustrations and personal anecdotes have been used to convey the messages and lessons for achieving and promoting happiness, justice, equality, peace and a healthy environment.

Chapter 1

Patience, planning and persistence

$\mathcal{I}$ remember the early years of promoting International Men's Day. It was a lonely time as many hours were spent producing photocopies, stuffing envelopes with information on IMD and licking stamps. I remember using personal expenses to print bookmarks and jerseys, posting letters to political leaders who did not know me and to countries that I will probably never be able to visit in my lifetime. How can I forget my appeals for assistance being rejected by government officials? I still remember sending emails and faxes to established organizations that doubted the relevance and usefulness of IMD. How can I forget the condemning of IMD by a few men? I've distributed flyers on IMD to strangers on the subways in New York (USA) and the streets of Senegal (in Africa), Toronto (in Canada) and London (in England). I have also been promoting World Unemployment Day (http://www.unemployday.webs.com) and involved in other forms of activism.

IMD seemed more like a burden than a blessing. Some felt IMD could not survive in a calendar which is already overcrowded with noteworthy days of activism. I remember speaking to empty chairs and near empty rooms on 19 November. There was a disappointing public response as the first observances attracted only 5 to 10 persons. And, most of the times, members of my family comprised half the audience! IMD had a dim future and unlikely chance of survival. Yes, it was expensive and seemed like a waste of energy but in the long-term there were results.

Those early years were times of frustration, disappointment and doubt. My credibility and reputation were being questioned. My efforts were mocked. It's never an easy task to accept rejection or to encourage others to accept a new concept or different view of life. It's even more difficult to convince people of the need to change. Today, it's no longer 'I' or 'me' but 'we' and 'us' as many co-operative coordinators and willing volunteers from different countries have joined and are sharing in the promotion and joy of IMD.

Many of you who are celebrating or promoting IMD in your town, village or country will identify with some of my challenges but you must not lose focus. Some persons have felt similar to insurance agents selling a policy as they tried to convince others to accept International Men's Day. Often, when I speak to persons of the significance of IMD, they would nod and agree it is a viable concept worthy of being observed. Some of their comments would be—'Yes, we definitely need this in today's world', 'It sounds like a good idea', 'I will read more about it and get back to you' and 'I support this effort and wish you well.'

Some persons promoting and spreading International Men's Day have endured criticisms, insults, rejections and weak arguments. Persons, including myself, know about telephone calls, emails and faxes that were unanswered. Blank stares, apathy and negative responses are a normal diet for many of us involved in promoting International Men's Day. Despite encouraging feedback, few persons are brave enough to actually organize, coordinate or plan an observance or attend an IMD event. Some persons are not action-oriented and instead pay lip-service to this aspect of the men's movement. Others might view organizing or attending such an event as wasteful, burdensome and unnecessary stress.

But there is another side of the story, a positive side. The high numbers of visits to websites dealing with International Men's Day, indicate a search for solutions to solve problems and the growing awareness of this Day. It seems odd that in January or May, people would be visiting IMD websites and blogs seeking information. Why would someone, so early in the year, want information on a day observed in November? It would be more believable if they sought information on IMD in late October or early November. This desire to learn about International Men's Day is further evidence that this Day has unleashed powerful positive forces which are changing lives now and will continue to do so in the future.

The annual newspaper reports indicate there is hope and change occurring in our world. Since its inception, IMD has blossomed into a movement which promotes goodwill and positively transforms the lives of many persons. Every year I am overjoyed to witness and read testimonies of persons who genuinely believe that the observance of IMD has resulted in greater stability in their lives and guided them from darkness into light. We are witnessing a dynamic and relatively young movement.

There is considerable joy to receive a telephone call or email from someone who agreed to assist in mobilizing persons in their state, province or country. Such responses as 'How can I help?' and 'Yes, I support International Men's Day and will encourage others' are the passports needed to be involved in this worldwide campaign of change. Now is the time to decide on your priorities. Maybe it is time to reshuffle your priorities and this could lead to a better life for you and others. IMD needs you on its team!

International Men's Day could be seen as a tree that is growing. The coordinators must see themselves as the roots of the tree. They often remain hidden from the public but provide stability and nourishment to the movement. Observers and supporters comprise the trunk and branches which are necessary for the tree to grow. The flowers and fruits comprise the achievements of IMD. These fruits and flowers would include improving child-parent relationships, reducing or eliminating violence and producing ideal role models.

Weeds are hated by gardeners and farmers. My garden has flowers and expensive plants. One day a weed appeared and I was too busy to remove it. After a few weeks the weed produced a beautiful lilac flower. I transplanted it to a flowerpot and began to regularly water it. The weed thrived and produced flowers on a weekly basis. Visitors and neighbors admired the flower and wanted to know its name. They wanted to buy one at the garden shop!

Some of the critics of Men's Day will initially appear as weeds who are seeking to choke and destroy International Men's Day. Give them a chance and see if their intentions are sincere and genuine. Some of those who criticize your life and actions should be seen as that weed with the lilac flower. The weed was uninvited but eventually became part of my garden.

Persons have been wondering about the structure of International Men's Day. Some have found it strange that there is no headquarters, base, anthem, song, uniform, flag or motto. Others noticed that there is no ranking, leader, membership cards or badges. Furthermore, this global grassroots movement does not require you to sign a document, contract, pledge allegiance or recite an oath. IMD does not keep a record of members or the lives that have been brightened and restored. You are free to enter and free to leave. Some have entered the movement, made their contribution to IMD and then moved on.

A few persons have wondered why different websites are allowed and the reasons for the existence of differences of opinion among supporters of IMD. If you believe that creating a website in your language or dialect would be more effective, then feel free to use that medium. There are a few logos used by most persons celebrating IMD and you are welcome to design a unique logo that would attract more people from your city, village or country. For instance, a coordinator from the First Nations might want to use symbols from his or her culture to better highlight the importance of IMD. These are all possibilities which demonstrate the flexibility of this aspect of the men's movement.

The apparent weaknesses and shortcomings of IMD are actually its strength. The fewer restrictions, open lines of communication, absence of formal structures, less bureaucracy and acceptance of differences, have strengthened this movement. This certainly makes IMD more appealing and inclusive.

The fuel of IMD comprises a growing number of dedicated and humble persons who have volunteered their time and willingly sought to create a better world. The majority of these amazing persons have full-time jobs whilst others are either part-time workers or unemployed. Their genuine desire to assist is sufficient criteria.

Why would someone from a distant country or village be willing to promote Men's Day and not expect a salary or some form of recognition such as a medal, trophy or certificate? This shows the urgency of creating a safer, more caring world. Each supporter of International Men's Day is extremely valuable and serves to help spread this message of hope and optimism.

In 2009, a group of five interested persons (two from Australia and one each from United States, India and Trinidad and Tobago) modified and approved the 6 Objectives of International Men's Day. This ad hoc steering committee proved to be a powerful catalyst which contributed to the rapid spread of IMD. This energetic and diverse group fully understood this precious creation and did not want to limit the growth of IMD. The five persons of the group represented 5 fingers on a hand. This hand would reach out to other hands. The next step of the journey was the development of a global network of coordinators. In 2011, New York (in the United States) obtained additional assistance from Associate Coordinators and Assistant Coordinators. These phases and evolution of International Men's Day indicate the need to allow more voices to be heard in this movement for positive change. Indeed, IMD has emerged from its cocoon. It is like a beautiful butterfly which has tested its fragile wings and now confident it can fly with other butterflies.

Some have questioned the title of 'coordinator' and wondered if it is an appropriate word. This is a term that has been used to identify persons who are promoting IMD in their countries across the world. These persons are volunteers who are eager to promote the 6 Objectives of IMD. If you are not interested in using this title but eager to spread the Objectives of IMD and host observances, then you are free to refer to yourself as a 'promoter', 'organizer' or 'supporter'. Or you might decide not to use any title. This is a minor issue that should not lead to arguments. Similarly, every year there is a designated theme for IMD but you can choose a theme that might be more relevant or applicable to your workplace, community or country. Or you might desire to use a theme for more than one year. This is also acceptable.

Should the coordinators have any special qualifications? No. You do not need to undertake any special courses in leadership or management to have an observance of IMD. The 'qualifications' you need include a positive attitude, a willingness to assist others, and an understanding mind. Both men and women could serve as coordinators. Additionally, the physically challenged and the unemployed are serving as coordinators. There are some prisoners who are now role models and have been annually observing IMD within their jails.

Being a coordinator should not be a burdensome job or one that demands your attention for the entire year. Create a timeline which will show when, where and how you will begin planning the observance. The more coordinators in a country would definitely mean less planning for you. Contact coordinators from other countries and share ideas and seek advice.

International Men's Day can be compared to a relay race. We are running in a relay race carrying different torches or batons representing positive words: hope, co-operation, goodwill, equality, environmental protection, acceptance, health, honesty, justice, forgiveness, support, unity, peace and understanding. And each of these torches or batons must be safely passed on to the next generation who will continue the race.

The pyramid was one of the architectural wonders of the ancient world. It took many years to build and each block was important and needed to be perfectly cut to complete the elaborate structure. Similarly, IMD has been built over a number of years and each person, represents a block in the pyramid. It is important that each person views himself or herself as being perfectly fitted into our society.

If you have a group of persons interested in observing IMD, then registering as a non-governmental organization or charitable organization is an option that will help in gaining recognition. Additionally, this official and legal recognition would allow you more leverage in seeking financial assistance from the public and private sectors. This is important as sometimes a stipend is paid to a feature speaker, and there are additional costs for websites, telephone calls, faxes, printing invitations, rental of venues and refreshments.

How can you promote IMD? The internet is one of the most effective methods and persons have utilized Facebook, YouTube, Twitter, Hi5, blogs and websites. Short films, debates, parades, car or bicycle rallies, marches, public lectures, drama, poetry and art are some of the creative ways of promoting and observing IMD. Press releases in the local newspaper, interviews on radio stations and a television appearance will certainly help educate others on the benefits of IMD observances. Get the local school or college involved. These suggestions would allow persons of diverse talents and cultural backgrounds to participate in IMD.

Where did persons and groups obtain funding for such ventures? Submission fees of competitions often comprise part of the prizes. Government agencies, local businesses and individuals could be convinced to sponsor prizes or assist with costs.

It is important that you record some or all of your involvement in International Men's Day. Why? Other coordinators and supporters would be interested to know how they could continue your work and improve observances. Additionally, it is important that your efforts are preserved for researchers on gender relations, masculinity or the men's movement. Photographs, audio recordings and newspaper clippings could be placed on CDs and donated to libraries and universities. Recording your achievements, plans and thoughts in a journal, website or blog is also a good idea. If resources are available, publish a pamphlet or booklet with recommendations or observations from your IMD observances. A short video or film, recorded with a cellphone or camcorder will form part of a visual collection. Be proud of your accomplishments!

What is the best venue to attract persons? It could be anywhere and depends on your budget and target group. An observance for students could be appropriately held in a school hall. A lunch-time seminar in the office would educate co-workers. In the past, IMD observances have been held in parks, under shady trees on university campuses, in living rooms, libraries, garages, town halls and hotels. Getting the message to others is more important than the venue!

Should there be a formal program for the observance of International Men's Day? The answer to this question depend on the coordinator and his/her team or group. You can have a formal meeting with cultural events and motivational speakers or you might opt for convening an informal gathering and then encourage spontaneous discussion on topics or a theme.

Who should be invited to an observance of IMD? Anyone who is interested in creating positive and lasting change should be invited. Men, women, teenagers and children will benefit from IMD. The size of the audience is not important.

The more crucial issue at your IMD observance is that there is constructive dialogue and that positive change has occurred which would improve society. Use the opportunity to invite the mayor, governor, councilors and government officials who would be better positioned to promote IMD at a higher level. Supporters and coordinators of IMD should be humble, willing to work with other groups, individuals and movements that are also on this path to create a better world. Try to ensure there is diversity among your participants and audience and of course—avoid excluding any groups in society. Remember that even though IMD deals with serious issues the observances do not have to be dull and boring!

Providing tangible tokens or souvenirs for participants and members of your audience will also help convey the message of International Men's Day. Bookmarks, pens, jerseys, notepads, buttons, hats, pencils, stickers and posters could be distributed or sold at IMD observances. These souvenirs could have inspirational words, your logo or simply the words—'International Men's Day, 19 November'. One group produced a calendar for IMD and each month had uplifting thoughts and pictures with fathers, grandfathers and teenagers. Each picture had men in positive everyday situations—having meals with their families, advising their children and at work. Such ideas will ensure that IMD is not confined to one day in the year but seen as an ongoing activity . . . a way of living.

Rewarding persons who have been promoting and supporting International Men's Day will be appealing. On 19 November, coordinators might decide to present plaques, medals or certificates to outstanding persons in the community whose lives mirror the 6 Objectives of IMD. Anyone could be honored—a teenager who excels academically, a policewoman for assisting troubled youths or a single dad who is a role model for his children. This recognition of persons in the community or country will provide role models for the public.

Some persons and organizations have appreciated the importance of IMD and have been having activities a few days or weeks prior to 19 November. Is this permissible? Yes, the events and publicity in the days before or after 19 November certainly increase awareness of this special Day and its significance.

Some might believe that now the spark is burning brightly, we can relax and enjoy the continuous growth of IMD. We must not become lethargic but continue networking and telling others of IMD. There is a hymn which was rewritten as a motivational folk song in the 1950s—'Keep Your Eyes on the Prize.' A documentary series was produced entitled—*Eyes on the Prize: America's Civil Rights Years 1954-1964*, which dealt with the struggles and challenges of the Civil Rights movement in the USA. You must keep your eyes on the prize!

Has International Men's Day really crossed geographical, religious, ideological, political, cultural, and ethnic and language barriers? Yes. Is it celebrated by men and women of different ethnicities, abilities, ages and classes? Yes. Is this an exaggeration? No. In 2010, International Men's Day was observed by boys, girls, men and women in more than 40 countries including China, Canada and Argentina. Newspaper reports indicated a strong European presence as

Austria, Northern Ireland, Scotland and Lithuania joined these worldwide observances. Not surprisingly, Latin American countries as Cuba and small Caribbean nations as St. Vincent and St. Kitts-Nevis were also part of these global celebrations.

IMD has been moving at a pace which reflects its synergy. During November 2010 to March 2011, IMD gained new coordinators in Pennsylvania, New Jersey, Arizona and Alabama (in the USA); Mexico, Angola, Botswana, Belgium and Norway. This extraordinary surge was due to excellent networking skills. The slowly expanding global network of coordinators certainly demonstrates the dynamism of the movement which was observed in more than 50 countries in 2011. This is evidence that International Men's Day has won the public's trust partly because of the simplicity of its message and absence of rhetoric and jargon.

Tell your friends, co-workers, relatives and strangers of a Day which was once on the fringe and marginalized but is now in the mainstream. Tell them of a Day which was once unassuming and seen as the underdog but has now become a powerful undercurrent transforming lives, shaping our society and presenting new visions of a brighter tomorrow. Tell them to come aboard and share the prize.

Nobody, including myself, has a monopoly or control of International Men's Day. IMD belongs to the world. International Men's Day is a gift to humanity. It is to be shared. Anyone can observe IMD without seeking permission. In the 21st century, the men's movement has another opportunity to guide and shape a powerful movement for positive social change.

Chapter 2

Building walls and dealing with thieves and losers

In any language and country, the words 'thief', 'bandit', 'robber', 'killer' and 'murderer' will cause concern, anxiety or fear among law-abiding citizens. These thieves and murderers are associated with violent and anti-social behavior. Thieves are often portrayed with masks or weapons and lurking in the shadows to avoid the police and the public.

Are we thieves and murderers? If we verbally and physically abuse someone then we have stolen that person's love, trust and hope. Whenever we are jealous, curse, act deceitful or condemn others, we have 'stolen' friendships, 'killed' understanding and 'destroyed' tolerance. Negative actions destroy bridges of understanding. To regain that vital human bond of trust and friendship, there will have to be a time for re-building and repairing.

Our negative and destructive attitudes contribute to us being viewed as 'emotional murderers' and 'friendship stealers'. We often unknowingly kill faith and a spirit of caring and generosity. Whenever we cause pain and harm to innocent babies, children and teenagers we are 'robbing' them of a bright future and wholesome personality. How did some of us become thieves and murderers? Maybe we were victims of crimes and became cold and uncaring like these thieves and murderers. But we must not seek revenge and continue on this destructive path.

You might not be equipped to catch and judge the guilty. You might want to remove the masks of thieves and show them the better alternative of living. You might want to cleanse the guilty hands and minds of murderers so they could continue life without a stigma and guilty conscience. Indeed, you might want to remove former thieves and murderers from the shadows and return them into mainstream society.

Many of us know the importance of walls. Some cities have built walls to protect their citizens from intruders or to define their boundaries. Some countries have well-guarded walls to keep out immigrants. China is famous for the Great Wall and during the Cold War in the 20th century, the infamous Berlin Wall separated East and West Germany. Jails or prisons have reinforced walls and electric fences with razor wire to prevent prisoners from escaping. Homeowners have built walls or fences for privacy and as a deterrent to criminals and animals.

In our lives we have also built walls and erected fences. We have built strong emotional, psychological and spiritual walls to protect us from hurt, pain, doubt, uncertainty and fear. Sometimes these protective walls are compromised or destroyed and persons are exposed to humiliation, addictions, or become suicidal. Let us ask ourselves—Have we built too many unnecessary walls? Are we the cause for others to build walls? Are we unknowingly building walls? Can we be strong enough to break a wall to save someone who is crying for help? Can we recognize a wall? Have these walls made us cold-hearted and isolated from the suffering of humanity? Have we made ourselves prisoners within these walls that we carefully built?

International Men's Day can be that sledge-hammer to smash walls that prevent us from enjoying life and forgiving others. And, IMD can be a ladder to help you climb over a wall to help someone. IMD will encourage you to climb your enemy's wall to rebuild friendships. The 6 Objectives of International Men's Day can be compared to six steps in a ladder for you to climb over negative walls. There are three questions you can ask yourself—Could you identify walls in your life and others? Can you help rebuild someone's protective wall? Are you willing to destroy a wall that is preventing happiness and peace?

We all want to be winners. Nobody likes a loser. It could be a board game such as Monopoly or Scrabble, a card game or sports such as cricket, football, baseball or basketball. International Men's Day helps you to understand that life is also like the board game—Snakes and Ladders. Sometimes you will move up and other times you will be down.

It would seem strange if you were told that International Men's Day welcomes winners and losers. IMD welcomes those who are competing at home, in the community or at the international level. IMD welcomes those who are not among the winners, those whose names are not in the record books and did not win a medal or trophy.

Often the desire to be a winner is so strong that some persons cheat. We are all aware of various scandals facing the sporting world. These include the use of steroids, match-fixing and payment of bribes. Sometimes there is an ugly physical confrontation between opposing players or fist fights among fans.

Some of us dream of competing at the highest level. We might hope to represent our country in the Olympics or World Cup. We might want to establish a new record so people will remember our sporting achievements. And of course, we would be disappointed if we are not chosen for this level of sport or achieve a record.

Sometimes we witness sporting events that make us understand the true meaning of competition, determination and hope. It could be a fallen athlete who hobbles towards the finish line, a marathon runner who bravely continues despite being last in the race or a gymnast who falls but still completes the routine. The athlete, runner or gymnast who fails and is disappointed knows that the many years of discipline and training are now wasted and that there will be no medal or honor at the finish line. However, the spirit that IMD encourages—is to focus on completing an event and to eventually cross the finish line of life.

If only sportsmen and sportswomen are role models and a competitive sports attitude exists, then there will not be the holistic and balanced development of boys, men, girls and women. The competitive sports attitude may negatively impact on work and family life if it leads some people to believe they must always be winners. Such an attitude could be an obstacle for projects which require building a network of support systems. Women and men possessing other talents or who are living decent lives would be ignored. Even more dangerous is the situation when these sporting icons fail. What would be the effect on those who admired and respected these sporting heroes? Certain aspects of the personal lives of a number of the world's sports and political icons have made headlines and shocked many of us. While their indiscretions have become fodder for tabloids and radio and television talk shows, we need to remember that these guilty men publicly apologized for their actions. More importantly, most of the wives of these men forgave them despite intense embarrassment. This forgiveness and acceptance is the essence of International Men's Day.

It is important to put these few concerns in context and say that sport should not be condemned. Why? Sport has the potential to encourage friendships, teamwork, physical health, bonding between fathers and sons, and promote excellence among athletes. Sport should be encouraged as one of many life-enhancing roles. IMD supports fair and clean competition that promotes solidarity and fosters better human relations. IMD supports the striving for excellence and perfection. Undoubtedly, sport is a powerful medium to overcome barriers of class, disability, nationality, gender, age and geography.

Social service organisations as the Rotary, Kiwanis and Lions can help us become winners. Furthermore, religious institutions, non-governmental organisations (NGOs) and civil society can play a significant role in helping the marginalized and those considered losers in life. The need for networking cannot be exhausted. There is a need to strengthen the bonds of friendship and encourage the exchange of ideas and technology.

Each citizen who is mentally and physically fit should be involved in some form of worthy activism or voluntary endeavour. No activity is too simple, too insignificant and unworthy if it involves easing the burdens of another living creature. Each drop of sweat, every cent, every second spent in a worthwhile activity will surely assist in helping humanity and improving our society. Citizens must be taught to avoid postponing, until retirement or later in life, the decision to begin an activity that could save someone's life and increase happiness. Many underestimate the power of one person or group making a difference. The burden of the world must not be on the shoulders of a few humanitarians and philanthropists.

Yes, IMD is concerned with gradually mending the fabric of a torn society. If you lose a button from your shirt, the easiest option would be to find another button and sew it on your shirt. It is highly unlikely that a lost button means you have to make or buy a new shirt.

Chapter 3

Violence against the vulnerable and using your talent

$\mathcal{T}$he world is familiar with natural disasters as earthquakes, flooding, hurricanes and tsunamis. Many of us would remember the shock on learning that thousands of persons had lost their lives when natural disasters struck Haiti in 2010 and Japan in 2011. Sometimes precautions minimize or prevent deaths during these natural disasters. Are we prepared for personal disasters? Can we survive an emotional earthquake, spiritual hurricane or psychological tsunami? International Men's Day can assist in minimizing the impact of misfortunes such as failure, sickness, disappointment and death. IMD is always equipped and ready to help those affected by personal, political, emotional, social and psychological earthquakes and tsunamis. We are ready to help the grieving, forsaken and the emotionally hurt. We are ready to comfort those who face discrimination and pain.

The movie 'Avatar' deals with the clash of two cultures. The plot deals with some uncaring, military officers from Earth who violently clash with the peaceful indigenous inhabitants from Pandora. This Avatar battle is part of reality when we consider the ongoing gender war. We are all familiar with frequent clashes and misunderstanding which occur between boys and girls, and men and women. The annual observance of International Men's Day on November 19th seeks to build bridges between men and women. This special Day is to break down barriers of distrust, hate and enmity among men and also between men and women.

There is another example of the unfortunate clash of two cultures. On 11 June 2008 in Ottawa, Ontario, the Prime Minister of Canada issued a formal apology on behalf of Canadians for the negative impact of the Indian residential school system. During the 19th and 20th centuries, residential schools separated over 150,000 Aboriginal (or Indigenous) children from their communities and families. This was a government policy that sought to deliberately isolate Aboriginal children from their culture and language so they could be better assimilated into the dominant European culture in Canada. This cultural genocide was only part of the colonial tragedy, as many of these innocent children suffered emotional, sexual and physical abuse in the schools. Furthermore, they were inadequately clothed and fed.

The Aboriginal Healing Foundation is based in Ottawa, Canada. This group's mission is to honor survivors of Canada's Indian residential school system. This Foundation and similar groups have organized retreats, workshops and seminars for grief and loss, sharing circles, participation in sunrise ceremonies and sweat lodges. Visits to ancestral ceremonial sites allow spiritual connection to the First Nations.

The First Nations in the United States have been victims of a holocaust. The shameful stigma of imperialism includes stolen lands and animals and burnt villages. Furthermore these once free peoples were forced into reservations and soon became victims of alcohol and gambling. Can a broken diamond ever be restored to its perfect beauty? No. It seems impossible to correct these wrongs but International Men's Day wants to work in resolving this gloomy scenario.

The Australian government offered a similar apology to the Aboriginal population in February 2009. The thousands of children who were forcibly removed from their families and communities and forced to assimilate were known as the 'Stolen Generations'. Can a crushed pearl ever be returned to perfection? No. International Men's Day wants to try to care for these deep wounds of injustice.

Aboriginal, First Nations or Indigenous peoples have respected the environment and lived simple, humble lives. Yet, across the world these honest peoples and their ancient cultures have been treated as inferior and unequal. These are not the only instances. The suffering and loss during the gruesome Bosnian and Rwandan genocides in Europe and Africa during the 1990s also produced Stolen Generations.

How effective is an apology? How effective is the word—'sorry' to a people who have been oppressed, stripped of their culture, humiliated and killed? The power of an apology depends on the willingness of the victims or their descendants to accept it. Additionally, the power of saying 'sorry' depends on the nature of the person who says it. Someone who is forced to give an apology would have little or no effect on the victim or hurt persons. A sincere heart and repentant soul will produce a genuine apology and be accepted by a forgiving mind.

Alien invasions, UFOs and evil robots are often portrayed in science fiction movies and books as leading to the destruction of humanity and our world. Some persons have been confidently predicting the world will soon end. We need to stop worrying about the end of the world and a bleak future. Promoters of IMD are concerned about promoting peace in the present and being optimistic about the future. We must believe we can improve the present situation and thus create a brighter tomorrow. Life is too short for you to be unhappy or always worrying. You must seize every opportunity to achieve personal fulfillment.

What is the appealing offer which IMD makes to each person? IMD can be compared to a bank that is open 24 hours, every day of the year. When you benefit from IMD it's like withdrawing cash or taking loans and not bothering about repayment. Your deposits and savings at this IMD bank occur when you adhere to the 6 Objectives and tell others about this movement. Too often we are more contented with muddying the pond of life. IMD seeks to calm the troubled waters, restore the equilibrium in your life and ensure you have a clear perspective and greater appreciation of life.

Three years ago, I received an email from a gentleman who said that he took medication to treat mental depression.

He said that upon learning of International Men's Day, he gradually reduced his dependency on the medication. He eventually initiated an observance in his country and stopped his regular dosage. He told me that his relatives, doctor and friends were worried when he stopped his dosage of medication. The gentleman continued to have IMD observances in his country on 19 November. Such frank and sincere accounts are amazing. I never expected IMD to have such an impact on persons. IMD enabled this individual to overcome inner demons and liberate himself. This is one incident and I'm sure there are many incidents where IMD intervened and was beneficial.

I want to encourage doubters and critics to try our free product—International Men's Day. There is no need for a prescription. IMD is for the sick, healthy, beautiful, ugly, winner and loser. Try IMD for as long as you want and there is a guarantee there will be no negative side effects. If you are dissatisfied feel free to return it to us. This free trial offer has no expiry date!

International Men's Day has changed how men view sons and daughters, how men view other men, how men view women and how men view themselves. It's a re-evaluation of our identity and allows for a better understanding of society and our purpose in life. IMD has certainly modified gender relations from one that is antagonistic to one that is complementary and supportive. IMD provides hope and optimism. IMD encourages mutual respect and allows you to be more self-confident and regain control of your destiny!

Supporters and participants of IMD need to be the voice for the most vulnerable segment of society. There are countless children who are in the middle of custody battles of divorced or separated parents. Furthermore, believers in IMD need to reach out to those lonely children who are in orphanages and the neglected street children who spend their lives struggling to survive and begging for food and money. And, we must reach out to those children from poor families who are unable to afford education.

The children of this world will certainly benefit from IMD. They will be able to differentiate right from wrong. They will be become upright and outstanding citizens. Genuine role models will emerge among children once there is proper guidance and a nurturing environment. IMD intends to support this favorable environment.

When I attended primary and secondary schools in Trinidad and Tobago (in the Caribbean), during the 1970s and 1980s, corporal punishment was a normal and accepted procedure. Disobedient students and slow learners would be beaten with whips made from tree branches, pieces of belts and rulers. Some students were insulted, slapped and hit by teachers. The classrooms became war zones. A few adults defended this excessive punishment by claiming it was necessary to create an orderly environment and ensure high academic standards of the schools. Few persons realized the irreversible and damaging impact of this form of punishment. The psychological and emotional trauma endured by these children and teenagers often contributed to cycles of violence. Some of those students, who were beaten by teachers, would later become juvenile delinquents or use violence to obtain obedience, respect and maintain control.

Not surprisingly, some of these abused students developed a hatred for education and schools, whilst others became dropouts or did not pursue tertiary education. International Men's Day cannot ignore any form of violence. Supporters of IMD must take a bold stance and strongly condemn violence against children, teenagers and adults.

How many times have we heard of a child who has gone missing? How many times have we seen the news of children and teenagers being the victims in murder cases? We do not know the child but we are concerned. Some of us would wonder—Who is to blame and how could society deal with this crisis? When will this madness end? International Men's Day seeks to address and prevent such scenarios.

IMD must be present in the life of the misguided teenager who is considering buying a gun to commit a crime. International Men's Day should be influential in the workplace and address the common problem of child labor as these innocents are overworked and underpaid. Participants and supporters of IMD should be concerned about child soldiers in global conflicts. I find it most appalling that some of the world's children are forced to carry weapons, are exposed to killings in the war zones and injured in battles. This traumatic situation will forever scar a child. Children and teenagers should never be forced or allowed to participate in any conflict or war. Their entire concept of life, their innocence and happiness are immediately shattered in wars.

Also, children and teenagers with incurable diseases and those who are physically and mentally challenged, must not be left behind. IMD must also seek to highlight positive role models—the children and teenagers who are respectful to parents, disciplined and talented in sport, art, music and academics. The privileged children and teens must be encouraged to help disadvantaged and troublesome peers.

Some people believe it is useless to attempt to rectify these negative situations because there will always be social problems, evil and sadness in this world. This is the wrong approach. Our children and teenagers must be protected and properly nurtured. Those who have strayed must be gently guided to the right path and embraced. All children and teenagers represent our present and future. International Men's Day must develop the ability to turn the tears of sadness of our teens and children into tears of joy and happiness. We must replace their emotional and psychological scars with pleasant memories.

In the first decade of the 21st century, two of the popular television shows in the USA were *American Idol* and *America's Got Talent*. Hundreds of interested persons auditioned in the hope of being selected for these television shows which attracted millions of viewers. There are lessons in these shows which can be applied to International Men's Day.

Ask yourselves these questions—Who is your idol? Are your parents or grandparents the idols in your life? Why is your dad your idol? Maybe he is a caring person who is faithful to your mom, helps you with your homework or teaches you how to improve in sports. Is your mom your idol? Maybe she offers wise advice or cares for you during sickness. Some persons have an older brother or sister who is their idol. You should also be aware that you could be the idol in someone's life. If you are teacher then some of your students will see you as their idol and some may wish to be a successful teacher. A compassionate doctor or nurse will be idolized by patients whose lives are in their care.

You must realize that not all the idols in our society are ideal. A movie star, charismatic personality or famous singer who has committed a crime or is promoting violence would gain considerable cheap publicity. But he or she is neither a suitable idol nor a proper role model.

When we hear the word 'model' we think of men and women dressed in the latest fashions. Or it could refer to a hobby as building model trains or airplanes. A role model refers to someone who displays exemplary behaviour and a caring attitude. There are good and bad role models. If you want to be a role model—there is no form or application form for you to complete. I do not know of any university or institution which offers a course or degree entitled 'Become a Positive Role Model.' Being a role model is not a genetic trait. You cannot watch babies and confidently make the statement—'That baby will later become a positive role model.' Anyone can be a role model. We must understand that we all have the potential, ability and talent to be positive role models.

A caring father automatically becomes a positive role model for his children, relatives and neighbors. He is not paid by anyone to be a positive role model. An honest politician automatically becomes a positive role model for citizens and other politicians. Both persons are role models and might not be aware that they are perceived by society as positive role models. A former drug addict or recovering alcoholic could be positive role models for persons seeking to rid themselves of their heavy chains of addiction.

Often a positive role model will not be rewarded, praised or given publicity. Are you pretending to be a positive role model merely for praise, to win friends and cheap publicity? Have you become a role model because of your genuine actions, views and behavior? Are you a temporary positive role model? Are you a superficial role model? Positive role models contribute to society by attempting to solve or ease problems. Positive role models feel part of society and desire to improve themselves and humanity.

The risk of being a positive role model is that any mistakes or antisocial behavior will cause a fall from grace that will seriously damage your reputation and offend others. Thus, there is an urgent need in our world for positive role models who can identify 'right' and 'wrong', make responsible decisions, behave in a mature manner, speak rationally and act without harming others. A positive role model is not someone who is involved in raising money for a charity and also displaying 'road rage' when driving.

There are many responsibilities for positive role models. Are you willing to fill that vacancy of a much needed role model? International Men's Day exists to help you become a positive role model, to promote positive models and also transform any superficial role models to genuine models.

What is your talent? You might not be blessed with a perfect voice, the strength of an athlete or intellect of a scientist. Probably your present conditions do not allow you to develop or use your talents. We all have talents. Maybe you can memorize an old song which you sing for the elderly, or you have the ability to make persons laugh and prevent them from being depressed. Do not let your talent remain hidden—find your talent and develop it!

There is a dire need to formulate an agenda, based on morals and ethical principles, to serve as a blueprint for the progress of societies. Countries need to consider embarking on a path to reverse and curb destructive value systems that have gradually eroded family values. These anti-social actions are usually promoted in the media and involve the glorification of infidelity, violence and homicides. Does society perpetuate a violent male especially with the exposure of young minds to violent 'action' films, novels and computer games? We have been socialized into this mode of violence. Undoubtedly, we need to question our value systems which portray violence as an attribute of the 'real men'. It seems that males who are soft-spoken, conservative and unwilling to engage in violence are deemed effeminate, weak or abnormal by their peers. Furthermore, peaceful men should not be considered emasculated. We need to reprogram our minds to understand that violence is not the only option but merely the choice of least resistance by narrow-minded persons.

Democracy is being abused and a nation will suffer when there is a steady flow of unchecked information entering the homes and minds of its citizens. Should the government intervene or would citizens be rational and capable of identifying the 'good' and the 'bad' influences and make the right choices? The individual should have that choice and the government has a responsibility to inform the individual of the pros and cons of the choice.

Some persons have been wondering—When will International Men's Day reach its full potential? What are the signs that this Day is being observed by the majority of persons? Is this Day relevant to current problems facing our world? These questions can only be answered when we begin to use our talents and decide on our idols or role models. Our challenge is to be wise in selecting role models, become good role models for others and use our talents to improve the lives of the less fortunate.

Chapter 4

The owl, the ostrich and balancing the scales

*W*hen faced with danger, the ostrich is supposed to bury its head in the sand. Do we adopt this strategy when we are faced with problems? Do we hope that problems simply go away? Some of us know the image of an angry or wounded animal charging through the forest or jungle. Are we similar to this angry animal creating a path of destruction and not caring about the damage to others? Or can we be compared to the owl that is considered wise and thoughtful? Do we think of solutions and implement these solutions to solve problems? Are we rational and considerate in our speech and actions?

International Men's Day encourages you to be like the owl and also to be rational and display concern for others. Furthermore, supporters of IMD cannot ignore or run from issues and always avoid angry and wounded persons. We need to help those who want to be spiritually filled and those who are emotionally and psychologically hurting. IMD cannot isolate itself from the rest of society.

The excitement of IMD must not fade. Some have been part of IMD but soon became disappointed and disillusioned. Why? Maybe they expected IMD to immediately transform their lives. Others have reluctantly acknowledged IMD as another day on the calendar of special days and activism.

Whatever your input into IMD, you will receive the same in return. It seems that International Men's Day is not a fad or fleeting fashion statement which will soon diminish or end. IMD has Objectives that represent the core of this vibrant movement. There are no magic words to recite that will solve problems and IMD certainly does not have a genie to grant wishes. Thus, International Men's Day cannot guarantee that tomorrow will reveal a problem-free society. But, we can certainly work towards that goal.

This version of IMD is unique because women such as Geneuvieve Twala of Botswana (in Africa) have promoted this day and willingly participated in IMD activities. One of the major reasons for the success of IMD is the fact that women's groups have also embraced this day. Hopefully, girls and women across the world will soon understand that IMD will create better sons, nephews, cousins, brothers, husbands and fathers. Many women have realized that IMD is not about female - bashing and condemning feminists or womanhood.

Both International Men's Day and International Women's Day strengthen and empower men and women, but we must not allow women to portray men as the 'enemy' and vice versa. In the novel and movie 'Alice in Wonderland', Alice meets strange characters. During her adventures, she is often fearful, confused and unsure of who could be trusted. Today there are many wives, mothers and sisters who can identify with Alice. Unfortunately too many of our precious females live in fear of men, cannot trust males or are confused in relationships. The same can be said of our boys and men who sometimes are confused and fearful of females. Men and boys need to ask themselves certain questions in trying to resolve these situations and understand their roles and status in society.

The long gender war must come to an end. There has been too much sadness, single-parent families due to divorces and too many victims. Feminists and activists outside of the men's movement should not feel threatened by International Men's Day. They need to realize that IMD is another peaceful phase of the men's movement. Many of their goals are similar to International Men's Day which includes improving gender relations and promoting gender equality. The focus of IMD is on males and females. Yes, International Men's Day highlights the common bonds of humanity. Remind others of the life-transforming impact of IMD. This movement is supposed to generate positive forces and not promote divisions.

In 2006, I attended an academic conference at the Universidad Pedagógica Nacional in Mexico. After the conference I had a conversation with a passenger in a taxi. I began explaining International Men's Day and he was eager to observe the Day because he no longer cared for Father's Day. Why? He was diagnosed with AIDS and given one year to live. There were negative reactions from his family. His wife took their two children and moved to another neighborhood. His friends were ashamed of him. I told him about World AIDS Day on 1 December. He did not want to be reminded that he had AIDS. I told him that International Men's Day shares a similarity with World AIDS Day because both days seek to provide hope, eliminate prejudices and remove stereotypes.

International Men's Day should not be seen as competing with Father's Day or any other special day. This choice of 19th November, my father's birthday, reinforces the inseparable link between both days. International Men's Day and Father's Day should not be seen as separate or strangers. Indeed, International Men's Day can be viewed as a 'son' or 'relative' of Father's Day.

On Father's Day and International Men's Day we need to remember those fathers who lost a child or children in wars or crimes. We should also remember the fathers in prisons or correctional facilities who are unable to be with their children. Also, let us be mindful that fathers with adopted children experience the same joy as fathers with biological children.

Should we remember women on Father's Day? Of course. In single-parent homes, many mothers perform the role of a father to her son or children. For instance, some mothers will teach their son to play baseball or soccer, and carry him fishing. Many wives, mothers, daughters and sisters willingly support and contribute to the duties and roles of fathers. The close celebration of Mother's Day in May and Father's Day in June are additional reminders that the world's fathers and mothers are two pillars in our world.

Supporters and observers of Father's Day and International Men's Day should also honor those men who perform fatherly roles. For instance, male teachers and principals of schools often display fatherly concern for students. Likewise, policemen act as fathers as they protect the neighborhood, city or village. An outstanding labor leader who helped form trade unions or campaigned on behalf of the working class would be referred to as the 'father of trade unionism' and early political leaders who helped establish democracy in their countries would be referred to as founding fathers. Undoubtedly, International Men's Day is similar to the goals of Father's Day. These include celebrating men's positive contributions to society, focusing on men's health, promoting positive male role models and creating a harmonious society.

Some of us know about different scales. There are scales in the market or grocery to weigh foodstuffs or small animals. Some of us have bathroom scales to monitor our weight. Suppose there was an International Men's Day scale with the screen displaying the 6 Objectives, your happiness level and state of mind. If you were to stand on the IMD scale, would the pointer on the screen indicate that you are adhering to its 6 Objectives? Would the IMD scale indicate you are unhappy and sad? Would the IMD scale reflect that you are heavy because of your burdensome worries and fears? How would you react? Would you claim the scale is faulty?

If there are negative readings on the scale, we want to lighten those burdens. If you are already slim and light, we want you on our team to encourage others to begin a diet of wholesome enlightenment and empowerment that is essential for the body, mind and soul.

The image of justice is depicted as a blindfolded woman who holds equally balanced scales. IMD is also blindfolded and would not judge you on the basis of gender, political affiliation, ethnicity, religion, caste, class, disability, age or geographical location. Supporters of International Men's Day want to balance the gender scale and other scales in life to ensure the existence of equality, equilibrium and equity.

It is unfortunate that some governments offer either token support or ignore the problems facing men. There is a glaring imbalance in funding for women and men programmes. Often support groups and NGOs focusing on males receive little or no funding. Sometimes the legal system will deprive a father of custody rights. How can an underemployed father pay alimony or child support? Often troubled boys and men cannot find proper and professional counseling. Such complaints are regularly heard from some groups and individuals who have been annually observing International Men's Day. Who will provide comfort and healing for the bruised, scarred and broken minds? What corrective action is being taken to address this glaring imbalance? Are you part of the solution or part of the problem? These are the questions that must be answered.

We want to balance the scale of life to ensure your time in this world is useful, productive and happy. We want to ensure that the scale of life is balanced for everyone. We want to stand on the IMD scale with you and work to ensure there are always positive readings!

Chapter 5

Mission to include the excluded: Who creates change?

"Critics of International Men's Day want to know "which men" are being talked about. Is International Men's Day talking about Rich Men? Poor Men? Black Men? Brown Men? Indian Men? Men in the Global South? White Men in advanced capitalist countries? International Men's Day speaks to all Men—Rich Men, Poor Men, Working Class Men, Homeless Men, Middle-Class Men, Black Men, Brown Men, Indian Men, Asian Men, Aboriginal Men, Men in the Global South, Men in Third World Countries, White Men in advanced capitalist countries—and the women who love them." (A "Teachable Moment" on Men's Issues, *In Search of Fatherhood* Summer 2010, p.40)

These powerful words were written by Ms. Diane Sears, the United States Coordinator for International Men's Day. It aptly captures the inclusive nature of IMD. The special Day is <u>not</u> designated as International Poor Men's Day or International Chinese Men's Day. The important word in International Men's Day is **MEN**. And, what is more important is that children, girls and women are part of IMD. Maybe the term 'gender movement' could be used as efforts are made to reduce the gender gap and polarization between the men's movement and women's movement.

We need to remember that IMD is not a small party or private home owned by a few or one person. The gates and doors of IMD are open for all. We need to always be there at the doors and gates of IMD and ready to welcome men and women who are willing to assist with efforts to create a more caring and humane world.

IMD is open for everyone. Once we begin to exclude others the men's movement will return to its fragmented state and IMD will become stunted. A few years ago an elderly man asked if IMD is only for perfect persons who are blameless and faultless. I replied, "Then I am not worthy to be part of IMD because I have many faults." Once we can acknowledge our shortcomings then we can find solutions and be on that path for wholeness.

Some persons might use moral, legal and religious arguments to justify the exclusion of some men from the men's movement. This is certainly the wrong approach to promote unity and harmony. What would happen to the excluded men? They would continue to be neglected, form their unique movement or join a separate group. If they join or form a group or movement, this will exclude us. Thus, the divisions among men would continue to exist.

Why would IMD want to exclude men or boys who are different? The creation of the Equality and Diversity Statement, in 2011, was another visible attempt to reinforce the inclusive nature of IMD. Even if this Statement had never materialized, IMD should be interpreted as accepting everyone. Some will argue that including men with different lifestyles or belonging to certain professions would tarnish the image of IMD and send the wrong message. IMD does <u>not</u> promote any particular lifestyle or job as ideal, acceptable or the norm.

There will be no signs of progress if the men's movement sets 'straight' and 'gay' against each other or promotes judgmental labels such as 'normal' and 'abnormal'. Should we ignore a small group of men and women because they do not conform to the rest of mainstream society? Should we ignore this small group because they comprise only 1% or 2% of the world's population? If IMD excludes this group, then we must ask ourselves—Is IMD promoting unity? Once we begin to exclude some persons then in the future we will find reasons to exclude others. The killing of persons or denial of jobs because they dress differently or have alternative lifestyles, should be concerns for supporters of IMD.

Others believe that on International Men's Day, prisoners in jail would reflect on their wrongdoings and undertake soul-searching. Undoubtedly, we need to remember and rescue those men and women who are not empowered, feel worthless and appear hopeless. Men who are guilty of crimes cannot be shunned or alienated. Each must be embraced as we search for a solution. No person must be left behind. The prisoner, politician, pundit, and pauper with their shortcomings and faults are all welcome to participate in International Men's Day. One woman from Africa, in 2008, asked that I remember her mentally challenged son. It is these forgotten persons, the emotionally and mentally imprisoned, who must also be included in IMD.

IMD should be that haven for men who are marginalized, bullied, humiliated, ostracized, mocked and ridiculed. Even if it is only one day of the year (19 November), these excluded men must feel included, welcome and proud to be male. Again, I want to highlight a relevant statement by Diane Sears in her 2010 article, "International Men's Day provides a welcome antidote to the mixed signals about manhood and masculinity, disrespect, and lack of recognition that many Men throughout our global village encounter" (p.40).

A few years ago someone asked me, 'When will International Men's Day create change in this world and where is the evidence of change?' My reply was—'It is happening now. Look around you and you will see evidence of change. Small and positive changes are often difficult to observe and monitor.' Change within the men's movement is occurring at different rates and on different levels. We cannot expect everyone to share identical views, visions and perceptions. There will be diverse views as some are advanced and progressive in their thinking and actions whilst others are still learning and grappling with the direction and challenges of the men's movement and peace process.

Persons within IMD need to be mindful of the quiet forces of change and the persons initiating and guiding this change. Everyone can be a leader within IMD. Everyone has the potential to be an agent of positive change. You cannot be an effective force of change if you spend time criticizing and condemning. Coordinators and believers of International Men's Day must not wait for others to initiate positive change but realize that they are empowered to ensure that violence; injustice and inequality remain in the past and are not part of our reality.

Has anyone ever told you about a war being won without weapons? Do you know of any battle being fought without weapons? Do you know of a war without deaths or casualties? Your obvious and first answer would be—no. There are battles that do not need guns, knives, swords or nuclear weapons. Can there be a peaceful war or a peaceful revolution? It sounds contradictory. Yes, there can be a 'war' or 'revolution' that is silent and peaceful. For example, in the 20th century, Mother Teresa and Mohandas Gandhi fought peaceful wars in India. Their early struggles were seen as losing battles but in the long-term they were victorious.

Wars and battles are often glorified. The success and the joy of victory tend to be the stamp of approval for future conflicts. Indeed, the fate of the world seems to be determined by the winner of wars. Men and women are participants in these tragic encounters. The majority of the world's military and soldiers are men. Ironically, the international peacekeeping forces also comprise men. It seems a grand irony that war is often the excuse used by some persons to ensure justice and democracy prevails.

War brings only temporary peace. History reinforces this with its never-ending list of conflicts. History has continuously proven that revolutions, coups, revolts, violent protests—all bring sadness, unnecessary loss of lives and wanton destruction. Often the change resulting from violence is only temporary and at times there is a return to the original scenario or the situation only becomes worse.

My undergraduate European History course spans the 19th and 20th centuries. Some of the infamous leaders who were responsible for destruction and untold sadness in Europe during the 20th century were Adolf Hitler, Benito Mussolini and Joseph Stalin. Yes, all men! I asked my students—Is it possible to create a world without violence? Could you imagine a world without guns and soldiers? The students could not offer a valid reason or logical answer and some simply replied 'Violence will always exist'. This answer is a good method to avoid solving a problem. One student said I was a dreamer and envisioned a utopia which will never materialize. After class another student told me that eccentrics and idealists speak about a perfect society that will never be achieved.

These students were unprepared for my questions on violence and possible solutions. Some students felt they could only initiate change if they became the CEO of a large corporation or a political leader of a powerful nation. A few students soon understood that they did not have to passively accept the attitudes of an uncaring society. The problem of society is that society cannot solve problems it created.

Sometimes, we question the causes for the uncontrolled aggression and hate emanating from men and women. There is need for more emphasis on individuals who are compassionate caring and peace-loving. We need to reshape our value systems and be more sensitive to the needs of others.

Ask yourself some of these questions—How do I handle conflict situations? How do we separate the men from the boys? Am I a man or woman merely because I am physically strong, have a loud voice or can use force others to settle disputes? Am I a macho man because I regularly consume alcohol or smoke? Am I a man because I hold powerful positions in a male-dominated world? Let me pose some additional questions—Can men handle changing gender roles? Gentlemen what is your role in society? Where are your priorities? The answers to these questions will determine the direction of IMD and the future of society.

We have witnessed an alarming number of deaths—suicides and murders emanating from domestic disputes and family arguments. Too much blood has been spilled, too many lives shattered and too many homes wrecked. Males are often portrayed as perpetrators of violence and abuse in the home. We need to stop these stereotypes!

Supporters of International Men's Day need to genuinely believe in dialogue and diplomacy to create peace. Only then we could consider the reshaping of our society. It is a fallacy that violence is genetic and thus unchangeable. There are caring and responsible men in our neighborhoods and villages who attempt to resolve disputes and live a life of peace. Our society needs to re-examine ideologies, the socialization process and institutions which promote stereotypes and distorted images of violent men. We cannot continue using the yardstick of violence to judge our men and women.

Militarized masculinities develop in threatened and war-torn societies. Some persons have wished that soldiers and countries at war would stop fighting for one day—IMD. Some will try to justify violence whilst others will accept violence as normal in our society. What should be the stance of supporters of International Men's Day regarding violence? Is the killing of a person justified? IMD is against violence . . . all forms of violence. Violence breeds violence. Show me proof that war contributes to permanent peace.

We must ask the question—Would the world have been a better place if violent persons were aware of International Men's Day? Undoubtedly, International Men's Day needs to be circulated amidst the violent, radicals and extremists whose actions create injury, suffering and death. Acts of violence are sometimes the result of misinterpretation of religious texts, cultural misunderstanding, ignorance and hate. Violent persons are not a separate species of human beings. They are similar to us and society has to accept some responsibility for their actions and be part of the search for solutions. IMD is an attempt to find that elusive cure for the anger, rage, hurt and jealousy which continue to stalk our communities. The process of exorcism and healing must begin now! Within IMD we can search for and devise solutions to rid our neighborhoods of gangs and defuse violence in our schools.

In some countries, citizens are allowed to carry licensed guns. This is considered one of their democratic rights. It is debatable if a gun can solve a problem or offer you permanent protection. During ancient times, a shield and armor were important to protect a warrior from a lance, arrow or sword. What is the shield and armor in your life? Is it strong enough to protect you from emotional, spiritual and psychological enemies? Are you ready to let International Men's Day be that shield, armor or bullet-proof vest?

As a result of terrorist activity, often innocent persons are injured or killed. Furthermore, a country, ethnic group, sect or religion could be stereotyped as violent. For instance, extremist Christians, in India, who destroy a temple or mosque, might contribute to Christianity or India being given a negative label.

Despite the gloomy scenario of bloodthirsty and stubborn political and military leaders there are obvious signs of hope. There is more than a glimmer of optimism that the next generation will attempt to cultivate that elusive era of peace and harmony. There is need to emphasize that building and maintaining peace is more difficult than initiating or controlling conflict.

Promotion of a culture of peace demands persons of sound character who are willing to make sacrifices and undertake a drastic overhaul of society. This peace should begin in the homes and schools. Those persons supporting International Men's Day seek to transform the negative images of masculinity or femininity and restore the dignity and respect in the family and society. By informing your group, organization, government, friends, public institutions and neighborhood, the message can reach a wider audience.

In 2010 and 2011, there were political upheavals and social earthquakes in Libya, Greece, Syria, Bahrain, Jordan, Tunisia and Egypt. These eruptions were due to unemployment, corruption, autocratic rulers and inefficient public services. Such incidents provide evidence that the global IMD movement should not be limited to the issue of gender but include the improvement of international relations among world leaders.

Is it justified to have protests against a government guilty of corruption, ignoring injustices and poor governance? The 6 Objectives of IMD certainly do not encourage protests. However, non-violent actions or peaceful protests are sometimes deemed necessary to generate positive forces that will allow citizens to realize a better world. Leaders as Nelson Mandela, in South Africa, fought a long battle against apartheid and Rev. Dr. Martin Luther King, during the 1960s in the United States, fought against injustice, discrimination and oppression. In 2011, Aung San Suu Kyi, Nobel Prize Laureate of Burma, said in an interview, "What we are calling for is revolutionary change through peaceful means." Suu Kyi (known as the 'Lady' in Burma) is a founding member of the National League for Democracy. Her party was victorious at the polls but a military regime denied her party from taking political control. Her statement is a mandate for us to consider. The observances of International Men's Day reinforce our commitment to a non-violent revolution creating positive change.

There is need for gender-specific media programmes to educate the public. For example, there might be male teenagers who could become great chefs but their fathers, who believed that only females should learn to cook, discouraged sons from preparing meals. Secondly, the formation of anti-racist and anti-sexist groups in communities is needed. Those seeking change should not include male-bashing as this only makes men more defensive and intolerable to change.

By providing non-violent solutions, and emphasizing the benefits of peace we will assist in the creation of suitable male role models. We are part of a global battle to defeat stereotypes whenever we promote positive role models for children, teenagers and adults. When we arm ourselves with tolerance, understanding and peace, then we are ready to fight and defeat enemies such as hatred, gender inequality, poverty, prejudices, dishonesty and bigotry. Being part of International Men's Day is really being part of a peaceful war, without weapons, to help save humanity from persistent problems. It is war we cannot and must not lose.

International Men's Day is also attempting to stop and prevent wars. One war which is ongoing is the 'gender war' which has killed relationships and marriages and injured self-esteem. There is major recruitment campaign underway. We are looking for brave persons and volunteers to be among the ground troops, generals, medics and captains to fight peaceful wars. Secondly, we are recruiting peacemakers and mediators to intervene and stop the many wars in our society. Supporters of International Men's Day want you to join forces to help prevent a destructive war or win a war without casualties!

In our society with unbalanced scales of power, we need to be mindful of the values being internalized by males. If today's masculine identities cannot be separated from violence then masculinity will continue to be hollow and superficial. Yes, non-violent men are often scarce!

Instead of burying or cremating children and loved ones killed in wars, we must bury and burn our weapons. Instead of unearthing land mines, we must unearth our fears and distrust. Instead of testing bombs, we must test models of multiculturalism. Instead of destroying cultures we must destroy crime, corruption and pollution. Believers of International Men's Day must know that now is the time to wave the white flag of peace, declare a truce, sign peace agreements and offer a handshake. Only then would peace finally prevail.

We must be mindful that peaceful and positive changes will <u>not</u> occur immediately. IMD is one phase of a long journey of healing. The entire society will benefit from a more understanding and caring son, brother, nephew, grandfather, uncle, father and husband. Persons who have observed IMD were sowing seeds of acceptance, tolerance and peace. Those seeds finally grew into sturdy plants. The next generation of men and women must nurture these plants and ensure they continue to blossom and bear fruit.

Who are the agents of change? The agent of change could be a newspaper editor who decides to publish articles on stress among men or surviving a divorce. Or, it could be the television producer and radio announcer who decided to educate the public on health issues affecting men. This will enlighten the public and make them more aware of symptoms of diabetes, preventing cancers and coping with a broken relationship.

Maybe the agent of change is a devoted wife who cares for her husband who is recovering from illness or a serious accident. The teacher who spends extra time with a slow learner is also an agent of change. Similarly, the teacher or counselor who intervenes to prevent bullying is helping change the future. Is there a benefit? Yes. A student who is being bullied might be considering suicide or could develop low self-esteem.

Ordinary men and women perform extraordinary tasks, with little or no recognition, to ensure our lives are comfortable. For instance, at the end of a day, the owner of a bakery or restaurant might decide to take unsold items and freely offer them to an orphanage or the destitute.

You are also an agent of change. And, you need to ensure International Men's Day continues to be an agent of positive change in our world. Could one day in the year become part of a global movement? Yes it could. The annual observance of World Environment Day is part of the powerful environmental movement. Similarly, International Women's Day and Mother's Day are crucial components of the women's movement.

Persons have been trying to understand the manner in which one day can influence their lives. The following illustration would be helpful. We all have a birthday. This is the day which is celebrated in different ways and many of us are thankful for life and the day of our birth. After our birthday, we continue living. We do not die for one year and suddenly come to life on our birthday. Thus, every day is a celebration of life and birth. Similarly, International Men's Day is not for persons to be temporarily transformed, changed in their interaction and thinking for one day and then continue in their old ways until the next IMD.

IMD was not merely included on calendars to correct a gender imbalance. IMD has a deeper meaning. Some supporters of IMD correctly believe that the day not only contributes to the men's movement but also plays an important role in the larger peace movement. The success and survival of IMD depends on the ambitions and goals of the coordinators, supporters and participants. Those observing and celebrating IMD determine its current direction and future impact. IMD is not concerned with quickly spreading like wildfire to all countries but more interested in helping others and maintaining that spark of optimism among humanity.

There is something unique about the final three months of every year. It contains a considerable number of noteworthy days. Breast Cancer Awareness Month is observed in October. Not many persons are aware that a small number of men are also affected by breast cancer! Health is a concern for all of us and thus it is no surprise that 'Movember' was created. Movember, (a combination of the words 'moustache' and 'November') is an annual month-long event which involves the growing of moustaches to increase our awareness and raise funds for men's health issues. And, World Diabetes Day which affects millions of persons is globally observed on 14 November.

On 19 November there is International Men's Day and one day later there is the observance of Universal Children's Day. The world solemnly observes 25 November which is International Day for the Elimination of Violence Against Women. Many are aware that 25 November also marks the beginning of the global campaign—'16 Days of Activism for No Violence Against Women and Children.' These 16 Days which include World AIDS Day (on 1 December) and International Day of Persons with Disabilities (on December 3), ends on 10 December with the observance of International Human Rights Day. For citizens of the United States, the month of November is significant as it is Thanksgiving Day. This day is celebrated on the fourth Thursday of the month. Additionally, on 19 November 1863, President Abraham Lincoln delivered the famous Gettysburg Address.

The Western observance of All Souls' Day is on 2 November and follows All Saints' Day which is to remember the souls of the deceased. Another solemn occasion is Remembrance Day which is annually observed on 11 November. It is also known as Poppy Day, Armistice Day or Veterans Day. It is a memorial day observed in Commonwealth countries to remember the members of their armed forces who died on duty and marks the official end of World War One in 1918. Interestingly, Australia, a Commonwealth country, has a link with 19 November. On 19 November 1941, during World War Two, the HMAS Sydney was sunk off the coast of Geralton in Western Australia, and 645 men lost their lives.

Has 19 November become a 'teachable moment' in the world's history? The evidence seems to suggest that

International Men's Day and other days of activism are presenting 'teachable moments' and inviting us to create and be part of these 'teachable moments.' In November 2010, one of the IMD websites (http://www.international-mens-day.com) recorded 372, 920 visits. This was for one month! This is another visible indicator that IMD has earned its place among other important days of activism and is fast becoming the people's choice! The extraordinary nature of IMD makes it difficult to be classified as simply another day of activism on the calendar.

Not surprisingly, I've encountered persons who were unaware of International Men's Day and a few professionals who appeared eager to find faults in this global campaign. They never participated in IMD observances or were uninterested in the event. Interestingly, the lives and actions of most of these critics are consistent with the goals of IMD. Are these persons part of the movement being promoted by IMD? Yes. It's ironic that these humble, upright citizens are the very role models who need to be actively involved in IMD to positively influence others! If your life reflects the Objectives of IMD, then you are part of this global movement. The all-encompassing nature of International Men's Day means that you are part of an ongoing campaign for successful transformational change and unprecedented personal growth.

Chapter 6

Eradicating injustice and inequality: Are you are a citizen of the world?

In July 2008, then presidential candidate of the USA, Barack Obama, speaking in Germany, referred to himself as 'a fellow citizen of the world.' How many of us can claim to be a citizen of our world? What does it mean to be a citizen of the world? Being a citizen of the world implies a common bond with humanity. It means you are affected by positive and negative developments in any part of the globe. As a citizen of our world you have a responsibility to bridge the divide between developed and developing countries. If we were all responsible and caring citizens of the world then there would be an absence of bigotry and xenophobia. As a citizen of the world you have rights and should not display religious fanaticism. Why would you want to embarrass, injure or insult fellow global citizens? International Men's Day hopes to be the passport that will guarantee you global citizenship in a global village.

Volunteers and well-wishers of International Men's Day are regularly devising strategies and supporting a global community that is more collaborative and less aggressive. International Men's Day is not a top-down movement. It has slowly spread from the bottom-up and maintained its growth among the grassroots. International Men's Day has challenged those who negatively view males and it has fought against stereotypes of men and women. IMD has confronted those who have trivialized the role of boys and men. Indeed, IMD is appropriately poised to challenge the future.

Two of the popular slogans in President Obama's election campaign were 'Change we can believe in' and 'Yes we can.' These are relevant in the worldwide campaign to spread the message of IMD. The question we must ask ourselves—Is International Men's Day creating permanent, positive change that we can believe in? When facing disappointments of small audiences or criticisms in promoting and observing IMD, you must think of those 3 words that gave hope to millions of Americans, overcame barriers and electrified huge crowds—'Yes we can.'

In 2010, International Men's Day was referred to as a 'Global Phenomenon' (http://blog.euromonitor.com/2010/09/african-male-consumers.html). This is certainly a grand compliment. Recently, some of my friends provided a feedback of the words they associated with International Men's Day. This included 'long-overdue', 'urgently needed', 'major change', 'positive campaign', 'interesting' and 'balance.' Their responses accurately reflect a movement and thinking which seeks to present another perspective of human relations and development.

In the past there have been many movements with charismatic leaders and large followings which began with lofty ideals but unfortunately these goals never materialized and the movements soon became derailed and lost their impact. The goals of International Men's Day have not yet been achieved. There is considerable work to be done and the journey is a long but rewarding one.

The global men's movement has been quietly experiencing positive vibrations. There is now more focus on the hidden goodness and untapped potential of our men and women who are urgently needed to create a harmonious world. The era of the blame game has ended. We must put aside our differences for a greater good.

The supporters and promoters of International Men's Day need to guard against the men's movement losing its momentum and energy. We have made tremendous progress and must maintain our path of healing, rebuilding and growth. The contributions of everyone are vital. IMD has struck a chord across a wide cross-section of society including governments, anti-war organizations, peace groups, feminists and academics. Hopefully, critics of IMD and the pessimists will eventually realize or accept the positive energies being released.

In the present and future, IMD should continue to be a grassroots campaign which will willingly embrace everyone. International Men's Day has the potential to become the global medium to heal our world. The concept and themes of this Day are designed to give hope to the depressed, faith to the lonely, comfort to the broken-hearted, transcend barriers, eliminate stereotypes and create a more caring humanity.

The reality of the world's present economic system is that it thrives on inequalities and unhealthy competition. There is a need to seriously undertake the challenge to reduce inequalities instead of believing problems are irreversible. Intellectuals and activists cannot keep accepting and believing that poverty, inflation and unemployment will always exist. Those in authority seem afraid to disturb the status quo by re-structuring certain aspects of the world's economic and political systems. Maybe they fear catastrophic repercussions.

Some persons have asked if International Men's Day is an ideology, movement or economic system similar to Socialism, Marxism, Stalinism, Leninism, Communism and Fascism which promised a new society. Many have written and spoken about a new world, different politics and a new religion. How have these promises helped humanity? IMD cannot be limited to an ideology, economic system or forced upon citizens. Instead, persons have the freedom to accept or reject IMD. Persons must have the freedom to create and shape their society . . . an improved society.

Current and past economic and political ideologies are nightmares which have failed humanity. The promises of equality, equity, justice and happiness remain as illusions. Possibly these are elusive because of the need for humans to have freedom and also the greed for an unequal share in natural resources.

International Men's Day is occasionally dismissed as not being a 'movement' or an 'ideology' because it does not adhere to the model or framework used by theorists and academics. IMD was not created to be a 'normal' movement that would fit nicely into the scheme of existing or past ideologies or movements. If IMD is restricted to a 'normal' theory, movement or an ideology, then it will suffer from shortcomings. Limiting IMD will reduce its potential and it will become like a caged eagle. Only when that eagle is freed can it soar in the sky and people will appreciate the grace and beauty of the majestic bird. Remember, IMD does not have prophets, ideologues and demagogues who spend hours debating and dreaming of a new society or proclaiming a new world. Instead, IMD is simply about finding practical solutions to everyday problems.

There is a need to develop new and more effective tactics, design better policies and monitor their implementation in an effort to eradicate socio-economic problems in all countries. Why must a developing country's currency be so devalued and worthless that its people are forced to sell body organs or become prostitutes? Why must thousands suffer and die because of a lack of basic medicine, clean water or food? Why were we apathetic bystanders whilst genocides occurred? Have we done anything to reduce human trafficking? Political and economic concepts and phrases are meaningless to the poor. The unemployed and the poor do not care about fancy economic terms or reports relating to the productivity of a country. One thought is on the minds of the sick and those in poverty—survival.

There is a need for developing countries to seriously assess their course of action. Why? Many are unwilling participants in an economic order in which the developed countries continue to dominate trade. Developing countries are given token roles and a voice but no power, and deceived into believing they will benefit. Poorer nations are hurtling headlong in a mad rush to embrace globalization without understanding the drastic implications on their economies.

The Great Recession, which began in 2008, had disastrous consequences. Millions lost jobs, money and/or their homes. Despite these unfortunate developments we need to be thankful for life. What are a country's most precious resources? Is it oil, gold, silver or manufactured products? Economists and accountants might say the strength of country depends on the exports, imports or budget deficits. The human resources of all countries are valuable and the most precious, that cannot be quantified, are the children and teenagers.

In ancient cultures, masks were worn by performers in rituals and ceremonies. During Halloween, Carnival and Mardi Gras, masks and costumes are worn by participants. Many of us have seen performers in plays wear masks to denote a certain personality or emotion. Superheroes and villains often wear masks and costumes to hide their identity. Some villains wear masks to hide scars. The comedy—*The Mask*, starring Jim Carrey, featured his amazing transformation and power whenever he wore an ancient mask. Sometimes wearing a mask empowers you and instills confidence.

Do I have a mask? Yes, I have more than one mask. Do you wear a mask? We all wear masks. What are these masks and when do we wear them? When we interact with our family we behave and speak in a certain manner. This would be different when we interact with co-workers or strangers. A horrible past experience will cause us to wear a mask to hide hurt, feelings of inferiority and insecurity or a broken heart. Some of us wear a smiling mask which hides sad and depressed feelings.

We might not realize when our masks are dirty, broken, sad or old. A few of us might not even realize we are wearing a mask or changing masks. The type of mask we wear determines the image we want to portray to others and often the public's perception of us. Some of us do not want to remove our masks to display emotional scars. Some of us only associate with others who wear similar masks.

International Men's Day will embrace you with your mask <u>and</u> when you remove it. And, if you want to wear a mask then we will take your mask and in return will offer you a clean and smiling mask which reflects a new and different individual.

Some politicians wear masks. During their campaigns they preach unity and present grandiose ideas merely to win votes. However, after attaining power they conveniently forget their promises and ignore the plight of their citizens. An overwhelming majority of the world's leaders are men and hopefully IMD will touch the lives of these political leaders and positively transform their values, intentions and outlook. Thus, IMD has the potential to enter the political arena and promote good governance, end civil wars, eliminate discrimination and allow for equitable distribution of resources.

Is it too much to ask that you should respect and accommodate different views? Is it too much to ask that you treat others with dignity? Is it too much to ask that you treat other persons as human beings? Is it too much for our political leaders to ensure education and health care are available and accessible for all human beings? Politicians who do not want a caring society would fear some or all of the Objectives of IMD. Leaders and governments who are oppressive, corrupt and uncaring would certainly be against International Men's Day.

For some persons, the danger of IMD is that it threatens to uproot the inequalities and alienation plaguing our society. Those who abuse the environment will see International Men's Day as a danger to their selfish interests. For a few, the danger of IMD is that it promises to shake foundations of stigmatization and discrimination. Some people believe IMD is the antidote for poisoned minds and the medicine which would ease the pains of the marginalized.

Chapter 7

Religion, racism, health and environmental protection

*T*he third Objective of IMD refers to 'well-being' and 'spirituality'. What does this mean? There are persons who do not believe in God or a Creator, or belong to the mainstream religions—Christianity, Hinduism, Buddhism, Judaism and Islam. Some believe in a spiritual life-force. IMD was never meant to directly challenge the religious doctrines, condemn religious texts or cultural practices. The inclusion of the word 'spirituality' is again another effort to demonstrate that IMD is inclusive and not designed to exclude persons who have no religion or different belief systems.

International Men's Day is not a cult and certainly not interested in brainwashing persons. We offer you a different view of life. If you decide not to accept IMD, then we respect and accept your decision. Those who are not supportive of IMD will not be deemed narrow-minded, inferior or backward. Any form of condemnation contradicts the core philosophy of IMD.

IMD cannot provide answers as to if there is life after death or the reasons for the existence of evil. But we can offer suggestions for a better today, brighter tomorrow and a safer future. We cannot suddenly create global peace but we are patiently and slowly transforming lives and appealing for justice. IMD does not have the power to suddenly make everyone happy but we are improving communication among peoples across the globe. IMD might not be judged a success but we will continue working to reduce barriers and empower persons. IMD cannot make inequalities immediately disappear but we will continue to work with others to reduce sadness and suffering. We too are also searching for answers and solutions—not temporary but permanent ones.

One of the major barriers to unity is the abuse of religion. There is a need for peace among the diverse religions, denominations and sects. For too long innocent persons have been killed, ostracised and scorned by others of different religious faiths. Over the centuries, millions of lives have been lost and psychologically scarred due to religious wars. The tensions are further complicated with fundamentalists and radicals claiming their actions are justified because it is done in the name of God.

Many persons need to be re-taught and re-socialized into understanding the fact that this world and humanity existed before organised religion. Furthermore, there is a need to be aware that religion was meant to improve and strengthen the relationship between humanity and God.

Instead, many unscrupulous persons use religion as a mask to accomplish earthly goals. It is unfortunate that in the name of religion many are oppressed, deceived, exploited, killed and condemned. Does God want or expect these antisocial actions? Some certainly act in a self-righteous manner as if God is bloodthirsty, revengeful and enjoys human suffering.

Some religious persons are concerned with saving the souls of so-called 'heathens', 'pagans' and 'idol-worshipers'. These upright persons offer a salvation which cannot alleviate poverty and pain. A few religious leaders offer useless rhetoric that cannot heal festering political sores and a crippled economy. Their pronouncements appeal to a gullible audience.

No religion or denomination is better than another religion or denomination. There is the ongoing debate as to which religion or denomination guarantees a place in Heaven, a better life after death, more happiness or a quicker path to enlightenment. The condemnation of atheists and agnostics by religious persons should be stopped.

Thus, in a genuine democracy, to embrace all of humanity there is a need to emphasize similarities rather than differences in the religious teachings. All non-believers, religions and sects must join hands and rid their hearts and minds of mistrust, petty jealousies and doctrinal squabbles.

Countries experiencing religious friction can take steps to defuse this tension by promoting inter-religious contact at schools, festivals, public sessions and private gatherings. Gradual and increasing awareness of various belief systems will sow the seeds of religious peace. Open-minded and rational persons must continue or initiate the dialogue of tolerance and acceptance.

We all know the value of health, life and car insurances. Insurance companies and agents are in almost all countries. International Men's Day is a type of insurance. How could IMD be seen as a policy to protect my health and well-being? Adhering to the 6 Objectives of IMD will help protect you from emotional, social and health problems.

Some persons might believe they do not need to observe International Men's Day because they are in perfect health and they have financial stability. These persons are in a comfort zone and possibly do not want to complicate their lives. Maybe they believe that only when there is a disruption in their lives that they should frantically search for a solution. However, IMD does not boast of quick-fix solutions. The change that is occurring is a result of commitment, open minds and a belief that persons or situations could be improved and positively changed.

One of the major differences between International Men's Day and insurances is that IMD is free. There are no monthly or yearly premiums and no penalty for stopping payments. So consider accepting a free IMD policy for you and your loved ones. This is a guarantee to keep you safe in a hazardous world. In times of disaster and misfortune, the 6 Objectives of International Men's Day will seek to restore equilibrium in our lives. Caring, dedicated and genuine visionaries are difficult to find but they are needed to help sell IMD policies!

A healthy mind and healthy body are promoted by International Men's Day. You don't need to be a qualified dietician, pharmacist or doctor to eat properly. Many of us are familiar with labels on foods and drinks but—do we understand these labels? Some companies attempt to promote healthy eating and bombard us with words such as—no preservatives, no additives, no coloring, 0% trans fats, 100% natural, organic, low in saturated fats, sodium free, no caffeine, zero cholesterol, no flavoring, no added sugar, high in fiber and rich in antioxidants. Undoubtedly, the world of marketing food is becoming more health-conscious. And, consumers now need to be wiser in making purchases.

Some of us are often confused by media reports claiming that a product such as hamburgers are healthy and beneficial to growth, but within a week there would be conflicting 'scientific' findings revealing how damaging hamburgers are to our body. It would be foolish for us to drink wine every day if a report indicates that red wine is good for the heart! It would be foolish if we ate chocolate four times a day because of a 'scientific' study that claims dark chocolate is rich in antioxidants.

We need to eat and drink in moderation. Only the foolish would celebrate obesity. It is an unhealthy condition that reflects poor eating habits, lack of exercise and/or emotional problems. Obese persons are not able to fully enjoy life and have a shorter life span than the average person.

Avoid the fad diets that are marketed as easy and quick ways for you to lose weight. Yes, you lose weight but in the process also damage internal organs and disrupt your body's metabolism. And, usually you gain the weight that was recently lost. Is your body obtaining all the necessary vitamins? Should you be taking supplements? Be careful because an overdose of vitamins is toxic.

Children with poor dietary habits will complain of tiredness and their physical growth will be affected. Furthermore, undernourished children will suffer from mood swings and low attention spans in the classrooms. Parents should not rely on school-feeding programmes to supply all the nutrients for their children.

Eat balanced diets with sufficient proteins, carbohydrates, fruits and vegetables. Your body type and work often determine the amount of calories you need. For instance, an adult construction worker or farmer will need more calories than a ten year old student.

We know the importance of exercise. You don't have to join a gym or buy expensive equipment to benefit from exercise. A simple walk, jogging or daily chores at home are all forms of exercise. Studies have shown that exercise also relieves stress.

Governments need to ensure there are sufficient advertisements encouraging persons to eat balanced diets and also provide healthcare that is accessible to those in poverty and residing in rural areas. The poor who are sick might not be able to afford medication or procedures such as dialysis or chemotherapy. Yes, we have heard that water is important for our body and we should try to drink 8 glasses each day. But, what about the poor and those in slums who receive no drinking water? What about those who are forced to drink dirty water to survive? Governments need to ensure a population has a clean and accessible water supply. Governments should also monitor the use of growth hormones in animals and harmful pesticides on fruits and vegetables. Such tainted foods will negatively affect those who consume them. Eating healthy, fresh and organic foods should <u>not</u> be luxury that can be afforded only by the wealthy.

You must be aware of methods to control or prevent non-communicable ailments as diabetes, strokes, high cholesterol, high blood pressure and heart attacks. We want you to be 100% healthy so that you can annually observe International Men's Day.

Another major challenge facing our society is the curse of racism. There is need for more racial and ethnic tolerance. One of the common traits of humans is the tendency to hate, alienate, condemn and destroy fellow humans due to physical differences. Belonging to a particular ethnic group is further complicated as this often means adhering to certain religious doctrines and/or cultural practices. Opposition and discrimination based on inherent physical characteristics must end.

The wounds of racial bigotry and ethnic strife are deep and far-reaching. Ethnic rivalry and caste prejudices are all responsible for untold suffering, sadness and loss of lives. Our world needs more positive voices and minds as a medium to transmit a message of understanding and peace among the various ethnic groups. If there is to be positive change, then an entire generation must be radically transformed in its mode of thinking and lifestyle. A simple act of being more tolerant in the workplace, community and home will not only positively influence others but teach children, the next generation, to love and not discriminate.

Why would persons feel IMD is a danger to themselves and others? Why would persons consider this Day to be irrelevant and useless? It is obvious that persons who are against International Men's Day would not appreciate positive role models, saving the environment or the true meaning of equality, freedom and justice. Undoubtedly, your support will assist in building a society aspiring for peace and a more understanding future generation.

IMD is not interested in continuing problems and promoting divisions. There cannot be compromises, temporary or limited unity. A country needs to be united at all levels. This should be a high priority for all nations. A united nation should continue the nation-building progress to the regional and international levels. We cannot boast of being united when individuality exists and there are civil wars, hatred among religions or senseless environmental destruction.

In 2010, there was a political tsunami when governments were embarrassed by the public exposure of confidential documents by WikiLeaks. This provided further evidence of the intrigue and deceit that exists among nations. Persons must stop blaming the 'West' or the United States for the world's problems. Developing countries need to also stop depicting developed countries as evil and immoral. Likewise, developed nations cannot continue to intervene in the political affairs of countries in the Global South and exploit their human and natural resources.

Unity does not necessarily mean residing in the same geographical region, speaking the same language or belonging to the same religion. In tackling obstacles and finding solutions there is a dire need for cooperation and collective work at the local and national levels. Citizens need to remove their blinders and adopt an open-minded, patriotic, pro-active approach to positively transform the family, neighbourhood, city, country and region. It is a gradual step-by-step process and consensus, though difficult to achieve, is important for positive change. If unity is absent, it is useless to attempt or expect a change. Rural and urban areas, poor and rich, Black, Brown, Yellow and White must unite to assist the oppressed, sick and hungry. We all belong to humanity's quilt and no nation, religion, class or ethnicity is superior or better than another.

It is essential to empower the poor with skills and initiate schemes to combat rural and urban poverty. Promotion of more grassroots organisations and the development of domestic and sub-regional markets will greatly improve the economic strength and exports of any developing nation. There is now a growing need for expertise to train and advise locals on strategies to boost private and public sector growth. The destiny of our world depends on the willingness of our people to initiate change.

It is unfortunate that every year, the earth is burdened by an increasing human population. It is not too late for countries to recognize the need for drastic environmental measures. There is an urgent need for our world to become more environmentally sensitized. Furthermore, improper disposal of hazardous substances, the release of toxic fumes into the atmosphere and creation of slums have a burdensome effect on the sustainable development of the planet. There must be the enforcement of environmental laws and stiff penalties to discourage abusers of the environment. Developed nations need to also accept the blame and must desist from blaming the developing countries as being solely responsible for the environmental degradation. Factories and individuals must stop using the oceans or other countries as a dumping ground for toxic chemicals.

Environmental issues such as endangered species, deforestation, global warming, climatic change, and protection of marine life, need to be regularly discussed in homes, offices and classrooms. Governments, the private sector and international organizations must increase environmental awareness programmes. Recycling should be a common practice among households and companies.

We are all familiar with a snowman and a sandcastle. Both are temporary. The snowman survives only during the winter and the sandcastle disappears after rain or a high tide. These have an important lesson for us. Are we going to create temporary change in our life or someone's life which is soon reversed? Or are we searching for a solution, an answer or change that is permanent? Are we sandcastles that crumble after the slightest rains and snowmen that quickly melt when the sun is hot? IMD is not about sandcastles and snowmen. This is a movement that is being built to withstand the strongest waves, heaviest rainfall and hottest weather!

Conclusion

The Future: Bright or Bleak?

*W*hat is your purpose in life? Are you a builder or destroyer? Are you self-centered and interested in promoting yourself or do you seek to improve the lives of troubled persons and assist the less fortunate? When you die, what type of legacy would you leave? Would it be a legacy of bitterness, disappointment, failure, shame and hate? Would you want to be remembered as someone who was violent or useless? Would you want to be remembered as a 'martyr' who caused innocent people to die? Would the world mourn for you or be happy that you are dead? International Men's Day wants to assist everyone in establishing a positive and lasting legacy. Your legacy should be one which will be remembered with a smile and kind words.

IMD must not only deal with promoting peace between men and women and within the family. IMD has a larger role to ensure the world is no longer deeply divided between the rich and poor, healthy and sick, Christian and non-Christian, East and West or North and South. This is

our world and **we** must ensure that <u>everyone</u> is safe, healthy and happy in our global village.

Let us imagine a world where IMD and International Women's Day were observed five hundred years ago. There probably would be less destruction of the Indigenous or Aboriginal peoples in the Americas and African slavery might not have happened or would have ended earlier. Additionally, if IMD existed five hundred years ago, society would have championed the rights of **all** girls and women to have opportunities to progress, access to education and be enfranchised. If International Women's Day and IMD were being observed globally during the first decade of the 20th century, then there might not have been World Wars One and Two. If IMD was being promoted there would have been more caring world leaders and citizenry who would have intervened to prevent the Holocaust in Europe and destructive use of atomic weapons. Today, we must appreciate the potential of such days in improving our lives, positively influencing those who govern us and preserving our environment.

Is IMD now in control of the global men's movement? Is IMD the authoritative voice of the men's movement? The answer to both questions is NO. International Men's Day never sought to hijack or gain control of the global men's movement. The men's movement existed long before IMD was conceptualized. Thus, IMD is part of the men's movement.

There is considerable reciprocity between IMD and the men's movement. Additionally, IMD does not enter into one-way relationships with individuals and groups. Participants and coordinators of IMD do not force men's groups and other organizations to observe this unique day. Of course, persons and groups who do not support IMD are neither ostracized nor alienated. Hopefully in the future, persons and groups who did not support IMD would be enlightened and embrace the benefits and advantages of IMD.

All voices within the men's movement are important and need to be heard. Furthermore, IMD has extended its outreach beyond the men's movement to assist other noble causes. IMD is certainly <u>not</u> about securing power, achieving fame or boasting of a large following. We must make genuine efforts to avoid divisions and fragmentation of the global men's movement. Only when we are united and enlightened, we would be empowered to assist and ready to embrace the rest of humanity.

Undoubtedly, in a united society we will be better equipped and positioned to eliminate or reduce evils as poverty, environmental pollution, unemployment and racism. Then we can boast of a healed world. International Men's Day must be the voice for troubled souls, the voice for the oppressed and the voice for the weak. IMD must listen and respond to the voices of the minorities. In this century and beyond, IMD coordinators and supporters must see themselves as serving the world.

The most difficult tasks seem to be promoting unity and becoming more understanding. It is very easy to destroy someone's reputation or gossip but it seems very difficult to praise someone or build a positive movement. It is critical that countries continue to send powerful and urgent messages requesting that differences and divisiveness be put aside and there be unity to combat the multitude of problems facing us. Tribal chiefs, mayors, ambassadors, kings, prime ministers and presidents must be encouraged and assisted in dialogue that will bring peace to neighbourhoods, towns, villages and nations.

In this era of globalization, rapid technological advances and space exploration, the poor and downtrodden of the world must not be forgotten. Now is the time for each person to embrace and adopt a philosophy of caring. It is time to join minds and hearts to develop a stronger international network to alleviate and eradicate the problems facing humanity.

Each individual has a role to play, be it policy-maker, politician, researcher, activist, student, religious leader, office worker, unemployed, vendor, insurance agent and academic. Each person must decide on his or her role because there is too much useless talk and wasted hours at conferences, committees, seminars and workshops. New terminology, speeches, commissions and grandiose ideas of alternative economic or political systems have not benefited the masses. Now is the time for direct action and visible results. Ideas and plans need to be properly assessed, enforced and monitored. We need to take action to ensure ideas; slogans and dreams become a reality. Obviously, change will occur when we stop useless talking and become action-oriented. The ultimate challenge of the new millennium is to effectively utilize the world's severely limited resources to alleviate the depressing and disturbing situations that confront more than half of the world's population.

There is still a monumental task ahead. There is a need to include the persons without access to internet facilities. Some might be wondering if International Men's Day will have any impact on the future. Others might wonder—what is the life expectancy of IMD? Will it end soon? I am certain that this unique day which is supported by men and women from diverse backgrounds will continue to grow and positively impact on our world.

Undoubtedly, future generations will be changed in their thinking, interaction and decisions. IMD will generate sufficient support which will be a wake-up call for the media and contribute to men and women being portrayed as honest, decent, morally upright, possessing morals and displaying integrity. More importantly, if IMD influences our world leaders and religious leaders, then there will be a noteworthy reduction or end to problems such as poverty, nuclear weapons, religious bigotry, unemployment, terrorism and racism.

Hopefully, there will be annual international gatherings where coordinators and supporters could meet, share ideas and discuss issues for *real* and *positive changes*. At these gatherings the future direction and leadership of the men's movement should be assessed. The convening of these meetings should be in different countries each year. Probably international organizations or wealthy individuals could assist in funding or hosting such a venture.

Persons are welcome to spread the message or pattern their lives on all or some of the 6 Objectives of IMD. How do they speak to your own experience? How could IMD touch the lives of more persons? How could you help IMD? Maybe in the future the global participants will decide to elaborate in more detail the benefits of the core Objectives to ensure IMD is equipped to better serve humanity.

Coordinators and participants must also appreciate the interconnectedness in our global village. Thus, coordinators should devise themes and deal with topics which are relevant to society. Themes and topics focusing on gender relations, masculinity/femininity, and fatherhood/motherhood are important. But also discuss and explore the linkages among gender, religion, class, ethnicity, poverty, media, environmental protection and nationalism.

A coordinator should not feel he or she is superior because he or she has been observing IMD longer than another coordinator or group. Likewise, participants and supporters should not believe their involvement in International Men's Day makes them better than non-observers or those who recently joined the movement. Participants and supporters must be empowered at the IMD observances. In turn, they would instill confidence, provide hope and support for others in distress and need.

Some would be hoping that in the future, every country would recognize International Men's Day. This would be ideal but any official endorsement from a government or international organization should not hamper the growth of this global campaign for positive, permanent change. For more than a decade, the continued support from millions of enthusiastic persons is more than sufficient proof of a unique Day which is vibrant, powerful and will continue to thrive. A solid foundation is in place for others to continue building and expanding.

In the future, more tertiary institutions such as Akamai University in Hawaii and Luther College (in the USA) and organizations as the All India Men's Welfare Association (AIMWA), All India Forgotten Women's Association (AIFWA), Positive Men's Movement of South Africa (POMESA) and the Association for Men's Rights (in Malta) must continue to be invited to be part of the IMD family. Existing networks must be strengthened and coordinators must continue and initiate global dialogue to prevent the men's movement from being fragmented and disjointed. The decision by groups to shift their Men's Day observances to November 19 was one of the strongest indicators of a spirit of willingness for unity and solidarity within the men's movement.

The decision to observe IMD does not mean that groups/ societies and individuals have lost their autonomy or identity. Also, observing IMD should not mean that groups/ organizations have compromised their goals or vision. The observance and celebration of International Men's Day should be seen as complementing and strengthening an organization's goals and individual efforts.

A relevant question we might ask now and in the future—has IMD failed because there are still problems as adultery, divorces, domestic violence and child abuse? The existence of these problems mean we have to work more effectively and work together to find solutions. We need to re-examine our strategies and devise new methods to cope with existing and future problems. We cannot continue to blame the past or others for these problems. The blame game must end! Undoubtedly, this is more than optimistic thinking and rhetoric, *it is a way of life that the next generation will nurture and continue to sow the seeds of peace, equality, freedom and harmony.*

Those seeking to improve our world urgently need the assistance of the media, government, NGOs, schools, religious bodies and concerned individuals. Only then would there be a chance for real change. IMD must be a period of enlightenment and we must emerge as dynamic warriors with a mandate to positively transform our society. Ours must not be merely voices in the wilderness.

Today we must start or continue the almost herculean task of cutting off the many headed hydra of crimes and hatred against humanity. The focus will be on the males and females and finding feasible solutions to the myriad of problems facing us in society.

There is no room for failure and we must continuing promoting constructive dialogue between both sexes for greater understanding and tolerance. Today we need to unite our forces and vow to never accept defeat. Let us join hands and hearts for International Men's Day to promote unity, resolve disputes, cultivate greater understanding between men and women, increase tolerance and thus create a safer, better world.